A Character Building Book™

Learning About Bravery from the Life of
Harriet Tubman

Kiki Mosher

The Rosen Publishing Group's
PowerKids Press™
New York

Published in 1996 by The Rosen Publishing Group, Inc.
29 East 21st Street, New York, NY 10010

First Edition

Book design: Erin McKenna

Photo credits: Cover, pp. 11, 16, 20 © The Bettmann Archive; pp. 4, 8, 12, 15, 19 © Corbis-Bettmann; p. 7 © Suzanne A. Vlamis/International Stock.

Mosher, Kiki.
    Learning about bravery from the life of Harriet Tubman/ by Kiki Mosher.
        p.   cm. — (A Character building book)
    Includes index.
    Summary: Demonstrates how bravery enabled Harriet Tubman, a slave, to escape to freedom, and subsequently bring more than 300 other people out of bondage.
    ISBN 0-8239-2424-6
    1. Tubman, Harriet, 1820?–1913—Juvenile literature. 2. Slaves—United States—Biography—Juvenile literature. 3. Afro-Americans—Biography—Juvenile literature. 4. Underground railroad—Juvenile literature. 5. Courage—United States—Juvenile literature. [1. Tubman, Harriet, 1820?–1913. 2. Afro-Americans—Biography. 3. Women—Biography. 4. Courage.] I. Title. II. Series.
E444.T82M67 1996
305.5'67'092—dc20
                                                                     96-6965
                                                                     CIP
                                                                     AC

Manufactured in the United States of America

Table of Contents

The Fight for Freedom

Harriet Tubman was not afraid to face danger. She fought fearlessly for freedom from **slavery** (SLAY-ver-ee) for herself and other African American **slaves** (SLAYVZ). In fact, more than 300 people owe their freedom to the bravery of Harriet Tubman, who led them from the South to the North, where African Americans were free people.

◀ *Harriet Tubman bravely led hundreds of African Americans to freedom.*

Slavery

Harriet was born around 1820. Her name was Araminta Ross, but she was called by her mother's name, Harriet. Like many other African Americans in the early 1800s, she was born a slave on a **plantation** (plan-TAY-shun) owned by white people. Slaves were people who were "owned" by other people. These people, often called "masters," forced their slaves to work long hours with little rest or food. Slaves received no pay for their work. They were beaten if they did not follow orders. Slaves were bought and sold like animals.

Slaves were forced to work on plantations like this one. ▶

Childhood in Slavery

Harriet, her parents, and her ten brothers and sisters lived in a tiny shack. It had no windows and no furniture. The family slept on the floor.

Harriet was only five years old when she was taken away from her family. She was put to work in the master's house, which had many windows and pretty furniture. Nobody showed her how to do her tasks. But when she did not do them properly, she was **whipped** (WIPT).

◄ *The shacks pictured here were the homes of the slaves of former President Zachary Taylor.*

9

Hardship

As she grew up, life became even harder for young Harriet. There was no time to play. She was fed just enough to stay alive. She was forced to work endlessly. She wove cloth, cleaned, took care of the master's kids, and worked in the cotton fields. Like other slaves, Harriet was not allowed to learn to read or write. And she knew that if she had children someday, they would be slaves too.

Harriet heard stories about other slaves who were struggling for their freedom. She knew that one day she would do the same.

Many slaves were forced to work long hours in the cotton fields. ▶

Slaves Fight Back

When Harriet was eleven, she heard of Nat Turner, a slave who led 75 slaves in a bloody **revolt** (re-VOLT). It was the biggest slave revolt ever. Everybody talked about it. Masters became worried, fearing that their slaves would turn against them. They made the laws for slaves stricter.

Harriet admired Nat and his fight for freedom. Her decision to set herself free only became stronger. But she knew that she could find freedom without hurting other people.

◀ *Nat Turner was caught before his revolt started.*
But his courage gave many slaves hope.

13

The Underground Railroad

Despite the strict laws, more and more slaves escaped to freedom. One master said that one of his slaves disappeared so fast, "he must have gone on an underground railroad." The "Underground Railroad" was a secret route followed by runaway slaves from the South, through the North, into Canada. People who helped the slaves along the way were called "**conductors**" (con-DUCK-torz). The homes that runaway slaves stopped at for food, rest, and a change of clothes were "stations." More than 70,000 slaves were freed through the Underground Railroad.

This slave traveled on the Underground Railroad in a wooden box. ▶

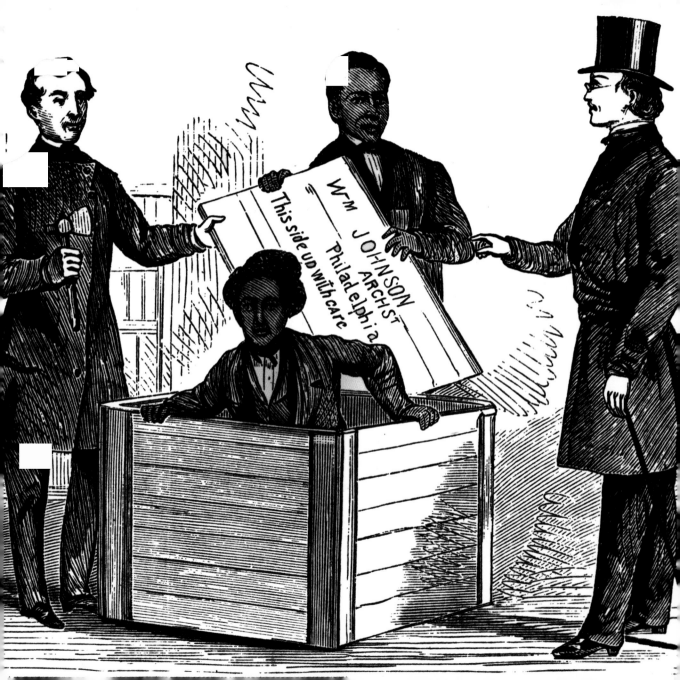

Hard Work

In 1844, Harriet married John Tubman, a free African American. In 1849 Harriet decided it was time for her to become free. She decided to escape through the Underground Railroad. With help from people who risked their lives, she bravely traveled from station to station until she reached Philadelphia, Pennsylvania. She was finally free.

But her family and her friends were still slaves in the South. She promised herself that she would make a new home and bring all of her loved ones to freedom.

Many slaves risked their lives for the chance to be free from being bought and sold like animals.

Life Up North

Harriet soon found work. She worked hard, night and day. But she was paid for this work. She had a clear goal: to become an Underground Railroad conductor. She knew that being a conductor was **dangerous** (DANE-jer-us), especially for a former slave. If she was caught, she could have been returned to her master. She would have been whipped. She might even have been killed. But Harriet was willing to face danger and trouble in order to rescue her people from slavery. She saved most of her money for trips back to the South.

Every time Harriet went back to the South, she risked being caught and put back to work in the ▶ *cotton fields.*

Working on the Railroad

In the years that followed, Harriet made 19 trips to the South and back to the North again. Every time she went South she bravely risked her freedom and her life. She brought more than 300 people to freedom. She led her family, her friends, and other slaves out of **bondage** (BON-dej). Harriet had them travel by night and hide by day. They became free thanks to Harriet.

This is one of the many families that Harriet helped to escape to the North. Harriet is the one on the left, holding the pan.

21

A Brave Fighter

Harriet was never caught. She was proud to say that she had "never run her train off the track, and never lost a passenger."

For the rest of her life, Harriet continued helping other people and fighting for good causes. During the Civil War, she worked as a nurse, a scout, and a spy for the Union army in the North. She fought for women's right to vote, helped raise money for schools for African American students, and established a home for elderly African Americans.

Harriet lived to be 93 years old.

Glossary

bondage (BON-dej) Slavery.

conductor (con-DUCK-tor) Person who runs a train. On the Underground Railroad, it meant a person who helped to free slaves.

dangerous (DANE-jer-us) Harmful.

plantation (plan-TAY-shun) Large piece of land on which a family lived and grew crops such as cotton.

revolt (re-VOLT) Time when people fight against the people who have power.

slave (SLAYV) Person who is "owned" by another person.

slavery (SLAY-ver-ee) Practice of allowing some people to "own" others.

whipped (WIPT) To be beaten with a belt or a long, thin piece of leather.

Index